The 1652 Country

Planning your Pilgrimage

A planning booklet for those intending to visit places of Quaker interest in the North West of England

2011 edition

Published by Quaker Life 2011
First published by North West 1652 Committee in 1995

Illustrations by Kenneth Mortimer Angus
Original text edited by Angus Winchester

Design by Quaker Communications
Friends House, 173 Euston Road,
London, NW1 2BJ
publications@quaker.org.uk
Britain Yearly Meeting is a registered charity, number 1127633

All rights reserved. No part of this book may be reproduced or utilised, in any form or by any means, electronic or mechanical, without permission in writing from the publisher.

The cover picture is part of a series painted by Kenneth Mortimer Angus (1884-1962) to celebrate the Tercentenary of the Society of Friends in 1952. We have endeavoured to contact the copyright holders without success. If anyone feels that their rights have been infringed by this publication, they should contact the Publications Manager, Quaker Books, Friends House, 173 Euston Road, London, NW1 2BJ.

Printed on recycled paper by Stephen Austin.

ISBN   978-1-907123-15-3

www.quaker.org.uk/1652

© Quaker Life, 2011

Contents

1. How to use this booklet 4
2. Pendle Hill 9
3. Brigflatts 10
4. Firbank Fell 11
5. Preston Patrick 12
6. Kendal Quaker tapestry exhibition 14
7. Swarthmoor Hall 15
8. Swarthmoor meeting house 17
9. Sunbrick burial ground 18
10. Lancaster 18
11. Other places to visit in the North West 20
12. A brief guide to further reading 24

1. How to use this booklet

This booklet aims to provide groups or individuals visiting the 1652 Country in North West England with basic, practical information which will help to ease the job of planning a visit and ensure that their visit runs smoothly. The booklet does not replace what has already been written about the 1652 story. Elfrida Foulds *The Birthplace of Quakerism* (1997 edition), remains the best brief guide to the sites and their history (though it is now out of print; a new updated version will be available soon). Ideally, you should be familiar with the outlines of the history before you begin to use this booklet.

The following material is built around the eight places which have traditionally been included in pilgrimage routes to the 1652 Country. For each place the booklet provides a brief summary of the events associated with the site, and practical details of how to get there and whom to contact to arrange a visit.

Planning your itinerary

These notes aim to help you journey through the 1652 Country. If you are coming on a pilgrimage as a group, large or small, **we encourage you to contact the pilgrimage secretary (contact details below) at an early stage in the planning process.**

Contact:
The pilgrimage secretary, Friends House, 173 Euston Road, London, NW1 2BJ, (tel: 020 7663 1007; email: 1652@quaker.org.uk)

The secretary will help you to co-ordinate your pilgrimage, ensuring that groups do not clash with each other. They may also be able to provide speakers to talk to your group, should you so wish, for which a charge of £25 (plus speaker's petrol) is made.

Maps: all the 1652 sites, except Pendle Hill, will be found on Ordnance Survey (O.S.) Landranger 1:50,000 map, sheet 97 (Kendal to Morecambe). Pendle Hill is on O.S. Landranger sheet 103 (Blackburn and Burnley).

The ideal pilgrimage route approximately follows the journey that George Fox made in the summer of 1652 when he encountered the Seeker community in Westmorland and neighbouring counties. In a matter of a few weeks he had gathered about him the body of preachers who helped to spread the Quaker message across Britain and overseas to Ireland, mainland Europe and America.

The key points on Fox's journey are **Pendle Hill**, where he had a vision of the people waiting for his message; the Sedbergh area (in particular **Brigflatts** and **Firbank Fell**) where he encountered the Seekers and convinced many people; **Preston Patrick**, where he spoke to another Seeker meeting and convinced many more; and **Swarthmoor Hall**, the home of Judge Thomas and Margaret Fell, where Fox was made welcome and which became effectively the headquarters of the nascent Quaker movement.

Many pilgrimages also include the following sites which, though not directly associated with the exciting events of the summer of 1652, provide much food for thought on the historic roots of Quakerism. They are **Kendal**, where the Quaker tapestry exhibition provides a wide overview of Quaker history; **Lancaster**, where many early Friends, including George Fox and Margaret Fell, were imprisoned; and **Sunbrick**, the Quaker burial ground near Swarthmoor where Margaret Fell and many early Friends are buried. A visit to Sunbrick burial ground forms a fitting and evocative place to end a pilgrimage. The order in which visits to Kendal and Lancaster are included may be varied without disrupting the story of Fox's journey in 1652.

In planning your route, don't try to cram too much into too short a time: space for reflection is central to the pilgrimage experience. Remember also that the roads in, and approaching, the Lake District National Park can be very busy, especially during weekends in the summer months, and congestion and delays can occur. Two possible itineraries are given on page 6; that for a weekend omits visits to Preston Patrick and Lancaster.

When planning your visit, remember to consider the desirability of taking out personal accident insurance cover, particularly for groups.

Suggestion for a weekend pilgrimage

Friday	pm	1.30	Climb Pendle Hill en route to accommodation
Saturday	am	10.00	Arrive Brigflatts
		11.30	Leave for Firbank Fell
		11.45	Arrive Firbank Fell
	pm	1.30	Leave Firbank for Kendal
		2.00	Arrive Kendal Friends meeting house
			Visit Quaker tapestry exhibition
		4.00	Depart Kendal
Sunday	am	09.30	Leave for Swarthmoor. Park at Swarthmoor Hall. Walk to Friends meeting house for meeting for worship at 10.45
	pm	12.00	Return to Swarthmoor Hall for talk/tour of house, followed by picnic lunch
		2.00	Depart for Sunbrick burial ground
		3.00	Depart Sunbrick for home

Suggestion for a four-day pilgrimage

(Note: morning times start from 10.15 or 10.30am and will usually finish at 12.30 or 1.30pm. Afternoon times start from 1.30 or 2.00pm and will usually finish by 3.00 or 4.00pm.)

Day 1	pm	1.30	Pendle Hill
Day 2	am	10.30	Brigflatts
	pm	1.30	Firbank Fell
			Preston Patrick
Day 3	am	10.15	Kendal (tapestry exhibition)
	pm	1.30	Lancaster (tour of Castle)
			Allow time for shopping / sightseeing in Kendal or Lancaster
Day 4	pm	2.00	Swarthmoor Hall and Friends meeting house
			Sunbrick burial ground

Where to stay

North Lancashire and southern Cumbria are popular tourist areas and include the busy holiday resorts of the Lake District and the coastal resorts of Blackpool, Morecambe and Grange-over-Sands. There is no shortage of hotels, boarding houses, Bed & Breakfast (B&B) and self-catering holiday accommodation to use as a base for visits to the sites of Quaker interest. Perhaps the most convenient locations to base a visit are places within easy reach of the main north-south transport links (M6 /A591) between Lancaster and Ambleside. Details of accommodation may be obtained from the **Tourist Information Centres** (addresses listed at the end of this section). The following is a list of specifically Quaker-related accommodation, some of which is simple, self-catering provision, that can provide an inexpensive base for groups of Friends.

Brigflatts (SD 641 912)
If accommodation is required in the Brigflatts area, please contact the warden (tel: 01539 620005), who may be able to make some suggestions. A self-catering cottage near Firbank Fell is available to rent from Nick and Janet Chetwood (tel: 01539 621715; web: www.ghyll-stile-mill-cottage.co.uk; email: janetghyll@aol.com).

Glenthorne, Grasmere (NY 336 076)
Quaker Guest house (full board or B&B) in the centre of the Lake District, conveniently placed in 1652 Country. Contact the managers (tel / fax: 01539 435389; web: www.glenthorne.org; email: info@glenthorne.org).

Rookhow, Rusland (SD 332 895)
Self-catering accommodation for groups of up to 20 in a former barn, next to the meeting house. Contact the warden, Robert Straughton (tel: 01229 860231; web: www.rookhowcentre.co.uk; email: straughton@btinternet.com).

Swarthmoor Hall (SD 282 772)
Three self-catering units (one suitable for those with impaired mobility) are available when not in use for the Hall's residential programmes. For details, see pp.15-16.

Yealand Old School (SD 504 744)
Simple self-catering hostel accommodation for groups of up to 25. Contact the wardens, Jim Jarvis and Beryl Mercer (tel: 01524 732336).

Further details of Hotel, B&B and Self-Catering accommodation may be obtained from the local **Tourist Information Centres** at the following addresses:

Clitheroe (for Pendle Hill): 12-14 Market Place, Clitheroe, Lancs., BB7 2DA (tel: 01200 425566; fax: 01200 414488; email: tourism@ribblevalley.gov.uk).

Kendal: Town Hall, Highgate, Kendal, Cumbria, LA9 4DL
(tel: 01539 797516; web: www.golakes.co.uk;
email: kendaltic@southlakeland.gov.uk).

Lancaster: Lancaster VIC, The Storey, Meeting House Lane, Lancaster, LA1 1TH (tel: 01524 582394; fax: 01524 382849;
web: www.lancaster.gov.uk or www.citycoastcountryside.co.uk;
email: vic@lancaster.gov.uk).

Sedbergh: 72 Main Street, Sedbergh, Cumbria LA10 5AD
(tel: 01539 620125; fax: 01539 621732; web: www.sedburgh.org.uk;
email: tic@sedburgh.org.uk).

Ulverston: Coronation Hall, County Square, Ulverston, Cumbria, LA12 7LZ
(tel: 01229 587120; fax: 01229 582626; web: www.southlakeland.gov.uk;
email: ulverstontic@southlakeland.gov.uk).

2. Pendle Hill • O.S. Landranger Sheet 103, Grid Reference: SD 805 414 •

The events of 1652
George Fox arrived in the Pendle area in May 1652. He was moved to climb the hill (which he did "with much ado, it was so steep") and, as he later recorded in his Journal, God "...let me see a-top of the hill in what places he had a great people to be gathered." From that point on, his mission seemed clear to him and he set off north towards the Seeker communities in the Sedbergh and Kendal areas.

Who to contact
There is free access on public rights of way to the top of the hill, so there is no need to contact landowners. If you wish to have a local Friend to guide you, contact Skipton and Settle meetings. (Telephone resident Friends, Skipton: 01756 793623; Settle: 01729 822313.)

Sawley Meeting House (SD 772 467)
Four miles north of Pendle Hill, is a convenient base to gather a party for an ascent of Pendle Hill. Contact the clerk, Wendy Hampton (tel: 01200 426266; email wendyfhampton@hotmail.com).

How to get there
By car: Pendle Hill rears up between Clitheroe and Burnley in east Lancashire and is a landmark for many miles around. The usual ascent is from the minor road between Downham and Barley (where there is a picnic site with snack bar and toilets). To reach this from the A59 (Preston – Skipton road), follow the signs for Chatburn village.

In the village centre, take the road to Downham, which runs uphill from the village main street. In Downham village, bear right just after the church. After crossing the stream at the bottom of the hill, bear left up a steep hill. Follow this road for two miles until you reach a crossroads, at which turn right towards Barley.

On foot: to climb the hill, park on the road side at SD 814 417, just uphill from the private occupation road leading to Pendle Side and Pendle House. Walk along the road to the gate on the right, just before Pendle House, Follow the well-marked path up the hill. The shortest ascent takes the steep, stepped path up the hill face. On reaching the break in slope at the top, turn left to the 'trig point' which marks the summit. A pleasant return may be made by continuing south from the summit and taking the well-worn track back down the hillside to the Pendle Side road.

The ascent is very steep. Wear good walking shoes or boots; allow plenty of time to gather your group on the top. The whole visit (ascent, time for reflection on top, descent) takes about two hours.

3. Brigflatts • O.S. Landranger Sheet 97, Grid Reference: SD 641 912 • www.brigflatts.org •

The events of 1652
It was in Richard Robinson's house in the hamlet of Brigflatts that George Fox stayed the night when he first arrived in the Sedbergh area in June 1652. The house still stands, though it is not open to the public it may be seen from the garden of the meeting house at Brigflatts. The meeting house, dating from 1675, is one of the oldest and most beautiful in England.

Who to contact
Contact the wardens (tel: 01539 620005; email: warden@brigflatts.org).

Opening hours: 9.00am to 6.00pm in summer; 9.00am to dusk in winter.

Meetings for worship: Sundays 10.30am with children's meeting.

How to get there
By car: leave the M6 at junction 37 and follow signs to Sedbergh. As you approach Sedbergh, take the A683 sharp right (signposted 'Kirkby Lonsdale'). Brigflatts is two-thirds of a mile (about 1km) along the A683. The hamlet with the meeting house lies off the main road to the left (signposted 'Brigflatts. Friends Meeting House 1675').

Parking: park in the lay-by on the right of the A683, opposite the lane down to Brigflatts.

Time Distances (by car): Pendle Hill: about two hours. Firbank Fell: 10 mins. Preston Patrick: 20 mins. Kendal: 30 mins. Yealand: 40 mins. Swarthmoor: one hour.

By train: the nearest mainline railway station is at Oxenholme (about ten miles). Bus services are not frequent and a taxi would have to be hired. The railway station at Garsdale (on the scenic Settle-Carlisle route) is about nine miles east of Brigflatts but is remote.

4. Firbank Fell • O.S. Landranger Sheet 97, Grid Reference: SD 619937 •

The events of 1652
An isolated chapel serving scattered farms stood on Firbank Fell until the 19th century. In 1652 it was used by the local Seeker community for their meetings. On Sunday 13 June 1652, George Fox was invited to preach to the Seekers there and in the afternoon preached from a rock on the open Fell side to "above a thousand people". Many were convinced and several of the Seeker leaders became leading preachers in the nascent Quaker movement. A plaque on a rock known as Fox's Pulpit, near the site of the chapel, commemorates these events.

Who to contact
Contact the warden at Brigflatts for further details (tel: 01539 620005; email: warden@brigflatts.org).

How to get there
Most visitors come to Firbank Fell after having visited Brigflatts.
By car: from Brigflatts follow the A683 in the direction of Kirkby Lonsdale for about one mile. Where the road bends sharp left at a junction, take the

right hand road (B6256) and follow this for about one mile until it joins the A684. The minor road up to Firbank Fell is directly opposite the junction of the B6256 and A684. It is steep and very narrow in places, but is passable by private cars and minibuses. Fox's Pulpit is about one and a quarter miles along the lane on the top of the hill on the right.

By coach: parties coming by coach should park in the lay-by on the A684 at SD 621 918 and walk up the lane to Firbank Fell. The walk takes up to 30 minutes in either direction. Alternatively, coach parties might consider hiring a minibus locally to shuttle them from the A684 to the Fell. Contact the wardens at Brigflatts (see page 10) for details.

Parking: space on the roadside verges is very limited. Groups coming by minibus may wish to seek permission to park in one of the fields near the Pulpit.

On foot: visitors are permitted to walk across the field from the road to Fox's Pulpit.

5. Preston Patrick • O.S. Landranger Sheet 97, Grid Reference (meeting house): SD 542 840 •

The events of 1652

On Wednesday 16 June 1652 George Fox was invited to another meeting of the Seekers, held at the chapel at Preston Patrick, the predecessor of the 19th century church (SD 537 835). A large number of Seekers from the surrounding countryside became Quakers and a meeting was settled here. Eight of the so-called 'Valiant Sixty' were from the Preston Patrick area. It later became the focus of the Wilkinson story controversy, a bitter dispute over authority in the Quaker church in the 1670s. The meeting house was built in 1691, but was radically altered during rebuilding in 1869.

Who to contact
For the church: contact the church office in Kirkby Lonsdale (tel: 01524 271320; office opening hours: Wednesday and Friday mornings), or contact the Rectory (tel: 01524 272044). There is no longer a resident vicar in Preston Patrick. **For the meeting house**: contact the clerk, Meg Hill (tel: 01539 561163).

Preston Patrick Hall (SD 544 837) A late-medieval manor house, it is a working farm containing a restored court room which is **open to Quaker visiting groups by arrangement only**. Contact Jennifer Armitage, Preston Patrick Hall, Milnthorpe, Cumbria, LA7 7NY (tel: 01539 567200; email: jda@pphall.co.uk).

Camsgill (SD 548 834) The home of the early Friends John and Mabel Camm and their son Thomas Camm, is **not open to the public** but is visible from the public footpath which runs past it from Preston Patrick Hall.

Meetings for worship: Sundays 10.30am (held at the meeting house).

How to get there
By car: Preston Patrick is close to junction 36 on the M6. Leave the motorway at junction 36 and take the A65 towards Kirkby Lonsdale and Skipton. A couple of hundred yards from the motorway junction is a second roundabout. Take the left turn here (A6070) towards Kendal. Take the first minor road on the right after passing under the motorway. For Preston Patrick Hall take the first turning on the right; for the meeting house carry straight on. It is the first building on the left.

By train: the nearest railway station is at Oxenholme, about four miles north of Preston Patrick.

6. Quaker tapestry exhibition and meeting house cafe, Kendal • O.S. Landranger Sheet 97, Grid Reference: SD 518 928 • www.quaker-tapestry.co.uk •

The events of 1652
George Fox passed through Kendal in 1652, preaching there as he moved west from Preston Patrick. A Quaker community soon grew in the town and became large, wealthy and influential by the 18th century. The present meeting house, built in 1816 to replace an earlier building, is home to the Quaker tapestry exhibition. Since 1994, a series of 77 embroidered panels made by 4,000 people from 15 countries, celebrating Quaker ideas, faith and practice in Kendal have been displayed here.

Who to contact
Contact the operations manager, Sandra Rose Timson (tel: 01539 722975; e-mail: info@quaker-tapestry.co.uk). Please make bookings for visiting groups of 15 or more.

Opening hours (2011): 29 March to 29 October, Monday to Friday 10.00am to 5.00pm (last admissions 4.00pm). The exhibition is open some Saturdays and some Bank Holidays throughout the season, but please phone or check the website for dates and times.

Admission charges (2011): Adult: £6.50 (concessions: £5.50). Child: £2.00. Adult with Toddler: £2.00. Family: £14.00. Group rate (for pre-booked groups of 15 or more people): £4.00 per person.

Exhibition facilities: step-free access to the exhibition and cafe; 77 embroidered panels; multi-lingual audio guides and large screen video; children's activities; interactive displays; workshops; gift shop; cafe and toilets with facilities for the disabled, children and babies.

Meetings for worship: Friends continue to worship in the meeting house on Sundays 10.30-11.30am and Fridays 12.30-1.00pm.

How to get there
The meeting house is in the centre of Kendal between Stramongate and New Road.

By car: Kendal has a one-way system: the yellow AA signs to 'Quaker Tapestry Exhibition' should help you to find the meeting house.

Parking: available at the meeting house (via Stramongate) or in nearby car parks of which the most convenient is multi-storeyed and accessed from Black Hall Road.

By train: take the Windermere line from the mainline station at Oxenholme. (Kendal is the first stop after Oxenholme.).

From Kendal station bear left then right to follow Wildman Street over the river bridge. After the bridge the road bears left, continue straight ahead and the meeting house is on the left.

7. Swarthmoor Hall • O.S. Landranger Sheet 97, Grid Reference: SD 282 772 • www.swarthmoorhall.co.uk •

The events of 1652 Country
In 1652 Swarthmoor Hall was the home of Judge Thomas Fell and his wife Margaret. George Fox arrived at the house towards the end of June. As a result of his preaching and discussions, Margaret Fell and her children were convinced of his message. Judge Fell did not become a Quaker, but allowed Fox and Margaret Fell to use Swarthmoor as a base for the Quaker mission of the 1650s. The house, heavily restored between 1913 and 1919, contains an important collection of 17th century furnishings as well as some furniture associated with early Friends. Since 1954 it has been in the ownership of London Yearly Meeting (now Britain Yearly Meeting).

Who to contact
The manager, Swarthmoor Hall, Ulverston, Cumbria LA12 0JQ (tel: 01229 583204; email: info@swarthmoorhall.co.uk).

Opening hours: the Hall is open for guided tours on Tuesday, Wednesday, Thursday and Friday afternoons at 1.30pm. Other availability is at any time that is mutually satisfactory to Hall staff and the pilgrimage; usually two days a week are set aside for such visits.

Admission charges: £3.50 per person (concessions: £2.50). Groups of ten or more: £2.50.

Individual pilgrims are welcome to contact the manager to arrange a self-guided tour with excellent taped commentary at any time of the year.

How to get there
Most visitors will approach Swarthmoor from the north or east (Windermere, Kendal, Sedbergh or Lancaster).

By car: take the A590 into Ulverston and follow the signs to Barrow, passing Booths supermarket on left, going over a pelican crossing, a roundabout and another pelican crossing and through the first set of main traffic lights. Turn left at the second set of main traffic lights, signposted to the railway station. After passing a big school on the left and a small one on the right, and going down a dip over a bridge, take the next right onto Urswick Road, then second right into Swarthmoor Hall Lane. After rounding a sharp left-hand bend, the entrance to the Hall is on the right.

By train: take the Barrow-in-Furness line from Lancaster and alight at Ulverston. On leaving the station turn right at the top of the station approach. The Hall may be reached by a footpath across the fields (**note: very wet in winter**) which is signposted and begins just before the primary school a couple of 100 yards from the station approach.

Swarthmoor Hall programme
Swarthmoor Hall runs a programme of events offering a unique opportunity to stay at one of the sites central to early Quaker history. Participants have exclusive access to the accommodation and to the historic rooms in the Hall. Some events may offer non-residential places. It is usually possible to have an (optional) guided tour during the course of your stay or to use the taped commentary to take yourself around.

The Hall can accommodate up to 17 people in single and twin-bedded rooms. It is also available for groups of people who might wish to organise their own events (such as retreats or workshops) on a self-catering basis. When not in use for programme events, the residential accommodation is available for holiday bookings and individual pilgrimage accommodation or B&B. It comprises three self-catering units of four or five beds. Two are family flats in a wing of the old Hall; the third is a ground level holiday flat with two rooms with twin-beds (National Accessible Scheme Level 2 – suitable for those with impaired mobility).

For further details of the programme or letting accommodation, please contact the manager (telephone number, email and postal addresses given on page 15).

8 . Swarthmoor meeting house • O.S. Landranger Sheet 97, Grid Reference: SD 283 769 • www.swarthmoorquakers.co.uk/swarthmoorquakers •

The events of 1652
The meeting house at Swarthmoor dates from 1688 and was converted from a building given by George Fox to the meeting of Friends who had met at Swarthmoor Hall since 1652.

Who to contact
The warden, Josephine Wyatt, 4 Rakehead Cottages, Meeting House Lane, Ulverston, Cumbria LA12 9ND (tel: 01229 580131).

Meetings for worship: Sundays 10.45am.

How to get there
By car: from Swarthmoor Hall turn left at the end of the entrance drive along Swarthmoor Hall Lane. Go straight over the crossroads into Meeting House Lane. The meeting house is on the left behind a high wall.

9. Sunbrick burial ground • O.S. Landranger Sheet 97, Grid Reference: SD 286739 •

The events of 1652
The ancient burial ground on the edge of Birkrigg Common, was first used in 1657. Among the early Friends buried there is Margaret Fell. Most Quaker visitors go to Sunbrick after Swarthmoor.

Who to contact
Access to the burial ground is unrestricted.

How to get there
By car: go down Meeting House Lane with the meeting house on your left (away from Swarthmoor Hall) to the T-junction. Turn right and follow the road out of town for about two miles to Birkrigg Common. After the crossroads on the common, take the road to the left towards Sunbrick. The burial ground is a walled enclosure with a linteled entrance, to the right of the road just before Sunbrick farm. (**Note:** large coaches are not able to negotiate the Sunbrick road.)

Parking: roadside parking is possible.

10. Lancaster • O.S. Landranger Sheet 97, Grid Reference (meeting house): SD 472 618 • www.lancsquakers.org.uk/lancaster •

The events of 1652
George Fox came to Lancaster in late summer 1652 and a Quaker meeting was soon established in the town. The present meeting house (parts of which date from 1708) replaced one on the same site (on the edge of the 17th century town) built in 1677. Lancaster's particular significance in early Quaker history lies in the presence of the county gaol in the forbidding Lancaster Castle. Many early Friends were imprisoned there, including George Fox and Margaret Fell.

Lancaster Castle

Who to contact
Mrs Christine Goodier, Lancaster Castle manager, (tel: 01524 64998; web: www.lancastercastle.com). Parties of over ten people should book in advance. Tours concentrating on the castle's Quaker connections are available.

Opening hours: daily tours (courts permitting) are all year, except Christmas / New Year, from 10.30am to 4.00pm. The tour (which contains reminders of the days of capital punishment) includes a visit to early cells similar to those in which George Fox was held.

Admission charges: £5.00 per head (concessions: £4.00 children, students and senior citizens). Ten or more booked in advance: £4.00 per head. Family charge: £14.00.

How to get there
By car: Lancaster Castle and the nearby Priory church (from which Fox was "haled out" in 1652) dominate the centre of the town and are well sign-posted. The castle is approximately two minutes walk away from the meeting house.

Lancaster meeting house

Who to contact
The warden, Strawberry Roth, Meeting House Cottage, Meeting House Lane, Lancaster LA1 ITX (tel: 01524 62971).

Opening hours: the meeting house and garden are open at reasonable times by arrangement with the warden.

Meetings for worship: Sunday mornings 10.30am and Wednesdays 12.30pm, followed by a picnic lunch.

How to get there
By car: follow the signs to Lancaster railway station; the meeting house is

next to the station (the town centre side) on Meeting House Lane. Access to the garden and the warden's cottage is by the cobbled driveway to the left of the building.

Parking: limited, but can be found behind the meeting house. (**Note:** parking is often full as the meeting house is frequently used by community groups.)

11. Other places to visit in the North West

Colthouse • O.S. Landranger Sheet 97, Grid Reference: SD 359 983 • Colthouse meeting house (built 1688) lies along the lane from the burial ground (SD 359 980) which was previously used for worship by Friends in the Hawkshead area. The stone seats projecting from the walls around the edge of the burial ground may still be seen.

Who to contact
Contact the clerk, Christina Birch (tel: 01539 436669; email:christinabirch@phonecoop.coop).

Meeting for worships (in meeting house): Sundays 10.30am. At other times contact the clerk, who will tell you where to collect the key.

Given reasonable notice, Friends from the meeting are willing to act as guides to groups wishing to visit the meeting house and burial ground.

Morecombe Bay: crossing the sands
The traditional route from Lancaster to Swarthmoor, used by George Fox, the Fells and other early Friends, was to cross the sands of Morecambe Bay. This was done in two stages, from Hest Bank (north of Lancaster) to Kents Bank (near Grange-over-Sands), and from Cark to Ulverston.

Visiting groups sometimes like to include a 'sands crossing' in their itinerary. For this, a guide is necessary: **on no account should you attempt to cross the sands without a guide.**

Who to contact
To enquire for a guide for the Hest Bank to Kents Bank crossing, contact the Tourist Information Centres in Lancaster, Morecambe or Grange-over-Sands. For the shorter crossing to Ulverston contact Ray Porter, 2 Next Ness Cottages, Ulverston (tel: 01229 580935).

Mosedale

A peaceful, simple barn-like structure, built (or converted) in 1702, lies on the eastern edge of the Lake District about ten miles from Keswick.

Who to contact
Contact the meeting house caretakers, Colin and Lesley Smith (tel: 01768 779397).

Meeting for worship: Sundays 10.30am from April to end of October (second and fourth Sundays only). (**Note:** Disabled access difficult. Wheelchair access to WC is not possible.)

Pardshaw • O.S. Landranger Sheet 89, Grid Reference: NY 103 254 •

Pardshaw meeting was the 'mother church' of the '1653 Country', those areas of Cumberland where George Fox encountered further groups of Seekers the year after his visit to North Lancashire and southern Westmorland. The meeting house was built in 1729, replacing one built 1672 on the side of Pardshaw Crag where Friends met in the open in the early days and where there is another 'Fox's Pulpit'.

Who to contact
Contact Christopher and Catherine Thomas (tel: 01900 822171).

Meeting for worship: 7.00pm, every third Sunday of each month.

Rookhow
• O.S. Landranger Sheet 97, Grid Reference: SD 332 895 •
In the lovely Rusland valley in wooded Furness Fells, the meeting house was built here, in 1725, as a convenient central point for holding monthly meetings.

Who to contact
Contact the warden, Robert Straughton (tel: 01229 860231; email: straughton@btinternet.com).

Meeting for worship: no regular Sunday meeting for worship.

Sawley
• O.S. Landranger Sheet 103, Grid Reference: SD 772 467 •
Attractive country meeting house four miles north of Pendle Hill, built in 1777 (replacing a building of 1743).

Who to contact
Contact the clerk, Wendy Hampton (tel: 01200 426266; email: wendyfhampton@hotmail.com).

Meeting for worship: Sundays 10.30am.

Settle
• O.S. Landranger Sheet 98, Grid Reference SD 818 637 •
Well-used meeting house (built in 1678) with a lovely garden, which can be used as a starting point for visits to Pendle Hill, about 20 miles to the south. Settle Friends are happy to act as guides to groups wishing to climb Pendle.

Who to contact
Contact the resident Friend, Alison Tyas (tel: 01729 822313).

Opening hours: the meeting house is usually open and details of how to get the key when the resident Friend is away are on the porch.

Meeting for worship: Sundays 10.30am.

Skipton • O.S. Landranger Sheet 103, Grid Reference SD 992 515 •
Attractive meeting house and garden, built 1693, close to the town centre (The Ginnel, off Newmarket Street). It can be used as a starting point for visits to Pendle Hill, about 18 miles to the south-west.

Who to Contact
Contact the resident Friend (tel: 01756 793623; email: skipton@quaker.org.uk).

Meeting for worship: Sundays 10.30am.

Yealand • O.S. Landranger Sheet 97, Grid Reference: SD 504 744 •
As the residence of Elfrida Foulds and, latterly, of Roger and Margery Wilson, the village of Yealand Conyers became a favourite base for pilgrimages from the 1950s. The meeting house, built in 1692, is next to the Old School, which offers simple hostel-style accommodation.

Who to Contact
Contact the wardens, Jim Jarvis and Beryl Mercer, (tel: 01524 732336; email: yealand@quaker.org.uk).

Meeting for worship: Sundays 10.30am.

12. A brief guide to further reading

The events of 1652 and the local history of the area are introduced in the classic booklet by Elfrida Vipont Foulds, *The Birthplace of Quakerism*, (Quaker Home Service, 5th edn. 1997), unfortunately now out of print. A new updated version will be available soon.

Most pilgrimage groups will find that the events are brought to life by readings from the words of George Fox himself in *The Journal of George Fox* edited by John Nickalls (London Yearly Meeting, 1975). An anthology drawn from all Fox's writings is found in Rex Ambler, *Truth of the Heart* (Quaker Books, London, 2001), which includes translation into modern English and an interpretation of Fox's thought.

Good starting points for the wider historical context to the rise of Quakerism are John Punshon, *Portrait in Grey: a short history of the Quakers* (Quaker Home Service, 1984); Cecil W. Sharman, *George Fox and the Quakers* (Quaker Home Service, 1991); Hugh Barbour, *The Quakers in Puritan England* (Yale University Press, 1964).

Modern historical interpretations of the origins of Quakerism include: H. Larry Ingle, *First Among Friends: George Fox and the Creation of Quakerism* (1994); Bonnelyn Young Kunze, *Margaret Fell and the Rise of Quakerism* (1994); Rosemary Moore, *The Light in their Consciences: the early Quakers in Britain 1646-1666* (2000).

David M. Butler, *Quaker Meeting-Houses of Britain* (Friends Historical Society, 1999) contains histories and architectural descriptions of all meeting houses in Britain. See also David M. Butler, *Quaker Meeting-Houses* (Quaker Tapestry, 1995).

Donald A. Rooksby, *And Sometime upon the Hills* (privately printed 1998), subtitled: *a guide book to places of Quaker interest in Cumbria, North Lancashire, the Yorkshire Dales and the Pennines*. Full of fascinating titbits of information; available locally and from Quaker Bookshop, Friends House, London.

Skipton
• O.S. Landranger Sheet 103, Grid Reference SD 992 515 •
Attractive meeting house and garden, built 1693, close to the town centre (The Ginnel, off Newmarket Street). It can be used as a starting point for visits to Pendle Hill, about 18 miles to the south-west.

Who to Contact
Contact the resident Friend (tel: 01756 793623; email: skipton@quaker.org.uk).

Meeting for worship: Sundays 10.30am.

Yealand
• O.S. Landranger Sheet 97, Grid Reference: SD 504 744 •
As the residence of Elfrida Foulds and, latterly, of Roger and Margery Wilson, the village of Yealand Conyers became a favourite base for pilgrimages from the 1950s. The meeting house, built in 1692, is next to the Old School, which offers simple hostel-style accommodation.

Who to Contact
Contact the wardens, Jim Jarvis and Beryl Mercer, (tel: 01524 732336; email: yealand@quaker.org.uk).

Meeting for worship: Sundays 10.30am.

12. A brief guide to further reading

The events of 1652 and the local history of the area are introduced in the classic booklet by Elfrida Vipont Foulds, *The Birthplace of Quakerism*, (Quaker Home Service, 5th edn. 1997), unfortunately now out of print. A new updated version will be available soon.

Most pilgrimage groups will find that the events are brought to life by readings from the words of George Fox himself in *The Journal of George Fox* edited by John Nickalls (London Yearly Meeting, 1975). An anthology drawn from all Fox's writings is found in Rex Ambler, *Truth of the Heart* (Quaker Books, London, 2001), which includes translation into modern English and an interpretation of Fox's thought.

Good starting points for the wider historical context to the rise of Quakerism are John Punshon, *Portrait in Grey: a short history of the Quakers* (Quaker Home Service, 1984); Cecil W. Sharman, *George Fox and the Quakers* (Quaker Home Service, 1991); Hugh Barbour, *The Quakers in Puritan England* (Yale University Press, 1964).

Modern historical interpretations of the origins of Quakerism include: H. Larry Ingle, *First Among Friends: George Fox and the Creation of Quakerism* (1994); Bonnelyn Young Kunze, *Margaret Fell and the Rise of Quakerism* (1994); Rosemary Moore, *The Light in their Consciences: the early Quakers in Britain 1646-1666* (2000).

David M. Butler, *Quaker Meeting-Houses of Britain* (Friends Historical Society, 1999) contains histories and architectural descriptions of all meeting houses in Britain. See also David M. Butler, *Quaker Meeting-Houses* (Quaker Tapestry, 1995).

Donald A. Rooksby, *And Sometime upon the Hills* (privately printed 1998), subtitled: *a guide book to places of Quaker interest in Cumbria, North Lancashire, the Yorkshire Dales and the Pennines*. Full of fascinating titbits of information; available locally and from Quaker Bookshop, Friends House, London.